Racism

Samidha Garg
and Jan Hardy

RSVP

RAINTREE
STECK-VAUGHN
PUBLISHERS
The Steck-Vaughn Company

Austin, Texas

Global Issues
Closing the Borders
Crime and Punishment
Exploitation of Children
Gender Issues
Genetic Engineering
Refugees
The Rich-Poor Divide
Terrorism
United Nations—Peacekeeper?

Published by Raintree Steck-Vaughn Publishers,
an imprint of Steck-Vaughn Company

Library of Congress Cataloging-in-Publication Data
Garg, Samidha.
Racism / Samidha Garg and Jan Hardy.
   p.   cm.—(Global issues series)
Includes bibliographical references (p.) and index.
Summary: Shows that racism has shaped our world historically and continues to affect the lives of people around the globe; also discusses the struggle against discrimination.
ISBN 0-8172-4548-0
1. Racism—Juvenile literature.
2. Race awareness—Juvenile literature.
3. Race discrimination—Juvenile literature.
[1. Racism. 2. Race awareness. 3. Race discrimination.
4. Discrimination.]
I. Hardy, Jan. II. Title. III. Series: Global issues series (Austin, Tex.)
HT1521.G35   1997
305.8—dc20   96-16163

Printed in Italy and bound in the United States
1 2 3 4 5 6 7 8 9 0 01 00 99 98 97

Cover picture
Celebrating the election of Nelson Mandela as President of South Africa in 1994

Title page picture
A school playground in London, England

Contents page picture
Cathy Freeman at the 1994 Commonwealth games

Picture acknowledgments
AKG London 10, 24, 38; Allsport 4 (Billy Strickland), 51 and *contents page;* Barnaby 14, Camera Press *cover,* 6, 9, 18, 20 (T. D. Jones), 21, 30, 34, 39 (Lynn Pelham), 40, 41, 53; Howard Davies 56, 57 and *title page;* Eye Ubiquitous 28 (Eric Miller), 33 (Eric Miller), 46, 49 (Matthew McKee), 50 (Matthew McKee); Hulton Deutch 12, 13, 25, 36, 37, 44, 45; Impact Photos 5, 15; Panos Pictures 9 (Penny Tweedie), 23, 32 (Eric Miller), 35, 48 (Penny Tweedie) 59; Popperfoto 16, 19; Topham Picture Point 7, 17, 23, 26, 27, 29, 31, 42, 43, 47, 52, 54, 58; United Nations 55.

Acknowledgments
For permission to reprint copyright material the publishers gratefully acknowledge the following:

The Independent for "Black Day for White Police" (November 1, 1994) by John Carlin; The Institute for Race Relations, 2-6 Leeke Street, King's Cross Road, London WC1X 9HS, for an extract by Jack Logan from *Patterns of Racism, Book 2,* an extract from *Sivanandan in Europe: Variations on a Theme of Racism, Race and Class* by A. Sivanandan, and an extract from *Inside Racist Europe* by Liz Fekete and Francis Webber; the *New Internationalist* for extracts from "Racism across the World" (No. 260, October 1994); Trentham Books for a poem by Pastor Martin Niemöller quoted in *From Prejudice to Genocide: Learning about the Holocaust* by Carrie Supple.

While every effort has been made to secure permission, in some cases it has proved impossible to trace the copyright holders. The publishers will make every effort to acknowledge these in subsequent editions.

CONTENTS

WHAT IS RACISM?

One race: The human race

Throughout history, there have always been some people who argue that human beings can be divided into different "races." These "races" were thought to be different not only in appearance, but also to have different kinds of characters and levels of intelligence. For example, in the eighteenth century, Carolus Linnaeus, a Swedish botanist, divided human beings into six types or "races." In the nineteenth century, Baron Georges Cuvier, a French anatomist, divided human beings into three distinct types in order of "superiority." Whites were placed at the top and blacks at the bottom.

In the late twentieth century, people have begun to understand more about the nature and role of genes in the human body. Scientists working in this area have shown that the idea that there are separate races within the human race is false. These geneticists have proved that there is a greater variation of genes within any so-called "race" than there is between one "race" and another. Despite this, some scientists continue to claim that they have discovered differences linked with race. In 1994, for example, two U.S. psychologists, Charles Murray and Richard Herrnstein, claimed in *The Bell Curve* that black Americans have a lower average

6 9

• • •

I am apt to suspect the Negroes…to be naturally inferior to the Whites. There never was a civilized nation of any other complexion than white, or even any individual eminent [well-known] in either action, or speculation. No ingenious manufacturers among them, no arts, no sciences. There are Negro slaves dispersed all over Europe, of which none ever discovered any symptoms of ingenuity.

Source: David Hume, a British philosopher, writing in *Gentleman's Magazine*, 1771

intelligence than white Americans and that this is, at least in part, due to genetic factors linked to race. But if nearly all scientists agree that "race" has no scientific basis, why does a belief in racial differences and racial superiority continue to shape societies around the world?

Being good at sports is not restricted to any particular "racial" group. In this picture, competitors run in the men's marathon in the World Championships held in Rome in 1987.

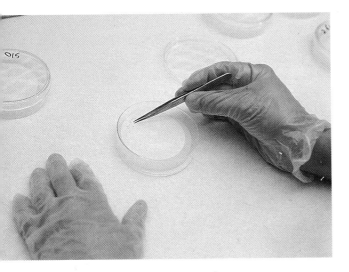

Genetic research in a laboratory in California. Geneticists have proved that there is no link between intelligence and race.

Racism

Although the term "race" has no scientific basis, the idea of "race" and of racial superiority is still used to explain and excuse the unequal treatment of one group by another. Racism can be explained as the way in which people from dominant groups in a society can exercise their power unjustly over others. Racist ideas are not just about skin color but also about other differences in physical characteristics, language, religion, and culture. These are all things that are important to the way people define themselves as a group. Jewish people, for example, suffer persecution in many parts of the world because of their culture and religion. The most terrible illustration of this was the Holocaust, when six million Jews were murdered in Nazi concentration camps (as were thousands of others, including Gypsies and homosexuals) during World War II.

"Racial" differences are not important in themselves. They become important when societies give them a social significance; that is, when societies value certain groups more than others. For instance, in many countries dark skin color has become associated with low social class and being poor. In many societies there is discrimination and racial prejudice against black and ethnic minority groups. When this happens, racism infects all aspects of society —government, the media, education, the legal system, and the economy.

The media and education play an important role in influencing how ethnic minorities are seen by the wider population. As children grow up, they learn

In 1995, lamps were lit on the railroad line leading into the former concentration camp at Auschwitz in Poland. This was to mark the fiftieth anniversary of the liberation of the concentration camps at the end of World War II.

about people around them from parents, teachers, and friends, and also from books, comics, television, and newspapers. Ethnic minorities are often presented in negative ways, including as a cause of problems. For example, until recently, movies have rarely presented Native Americans as fighting in defense of their land and rights but as savages attacking white people. Often, news programs in Western countries only cover stories from Africa and Asia when these involve poverty and war. Problems of rising crime in inner cities are often linked to the presence of large numbers of ethnic minorities living there, rather than to the economic conditions in such areas. Criminal acts by whites are often not covered by the media. Similarly, until recently, books that teach about racism were rarely found in schools. As much as people are influenced by education and the media, it is not surprising that a lot of white people hold negative and simplified views about ethnic minorities. Such views, sometimes called stereotypes, lead to racial prejudice.

A city street scene, North London, England, in 1995

Fact File

Racism in many places

Employment
Racism affects people's chances of getting jobs.
- **United States** Black people are twice as likely to be unemployed as whites.
- **Great Britain** Ethnic minorities are, on average, twice as likely to be unemployed as whites. For some groups, unemployment is four times as great.
- **Australia** Aboriginal people are more than three times as likely to be unemployed than the general population.
- **Canada** Indigenous Canadians are twice as likely to be unemployed as the rest of the population.

Racist violence
Racist violence is increasing in many parts of the world.
- **United States** In 1993, seven out of ten "hate" crimes were racially motivated—36 percent against blacks and 13 percent against Jews.
- **Great Britain** 90 percent of racially motivated attacks are carried out by whites against ethnic minorities. It is estimated that, in 1993, there were 130,000 racist incidents.
- **Germany** In 1993, at least 52 people died as a result of racist activities.
- **Italy** In the first nine months of 1993, one hundred racial attacks were estimated to have taken place in Rome.

Criminal justice
Racism increases the chances of people who belong to oppressed groups being imprisoned.
- **United States** Black people make up 12 percent of the total population but 48 percent of the prison population.
- **Great Britain** Ethnic minorities form 5.5 percent of the total population but 18.6 percent of the prison population.
- **Australia** The percentage of Aboriginal people in prison is fourteen times the national average.
- **New Zealand** Maoris make up 9 percent of the total population but 50 percent of the prison population.

Source: *New Internationalist,* October 1994

(Right) Many ethnic minority families face racial harassment and violence. This family was moved, temporarily, to bed-and-breakfast accommodations after a racial attack on their home in a housing project in London, England.

(Right) Right-wing extremists march through Dresden, Germany, in 1994, to mark the birthday of former Nazi leader Adolf Hitler and to celebrate racism and fascism.

Roots of racism

Racism has historical roots in European colonialism, which began over 400 years ago. This had far-reaching effects on the societies of many countries around the world.

Western industrial societies became rich because they were able to exploit many parts of the world. At first European traders took precious metals, cloth, and foodstuffs from Africa, South America, and Asia. Later, Europeans seized lands as colonies, traded in slaves, and put down rebellions by military force.

First, areas such as North America, Australia, and New Zealand were occupied and settled by Europeans, who largely destroyed the indigenous populations. These lands have been run mainly by white people ever since.

In other countries, such as South Africa and Zimbabwe, Europeans fought the indigenous peoples and took over many of their lands. The indigenous peoples were then employed as cheap labor on the lands that were once theirs. Until very recently, these areas were ruled by white minority governments, which used military power to maintain their privileged position.

In North America, during the nineteenth century, European settlers began to move westward, occupying large areas of land and driving out the indigenous American population. Here, a group of colonists arrives at a new settlement in the West in 1875.

Europeans did not settle in large numbers in countries such as India and other parts of Asia, Africa, and South America, but governed them as their colonies.

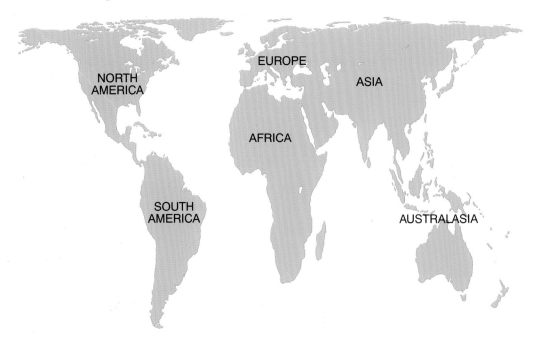

This map shows the continents in proportion to their land area.

In countries in South America and the Caribbean, the original indigenous populations were largely wiped out. They were replaced by slaves from Africa and, later, by hired labor from Asia.

European traders and settlers believed that they were superior to the people in the lands they took over, and they thought they could justify their behavior. Africans were packed into slave ships in chains, for example, and transported like animals to European colonies in the Caribbean and South America. At least thirty million of them died on the way.

Some nineteenth-century scientists believed that Africans were in fact just like animals, and they tried to prove that they were similar to apes. Ideas of white superiority became an important part of the way Europeans thought about the rest of the world. This way of thinking can still be found today.

66   99

• • •

But as they have been passing from creation they have performed their allotted task; and the fires of the dark child of the forest have cleared the soil, the hills and the valleys of the super-abundant scrub and timber, that covered the country and presented a bar to its occupation. Now, prepared by the hands of the lowest race in the scale of humanity…the soil of these extensive regions is ready to receive the virgin impressions of civilized man.

Source: Logan Jack, writing from northernmost Australia, 1922

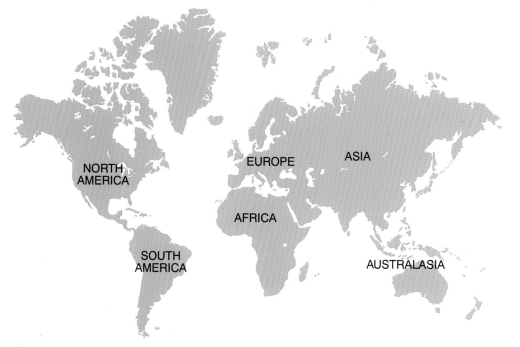

Even the maps we use suggest that Northern countries, where mainly white people live, are more important than Southern countries, which are populated mainly by people of color.

Racism lives on in the former colonies. For example, in some South American countries a light skin color is seen as a sign of social superiority. The black descendants of African slaves are often poor and remain the lowest class in society.

Racism and resistance
Throughout the periods of slavery and colonialism, the indigenous peoples resisted their rulers. For example, in Australia, the Aboriginal peoples fought a guerrilla war against the white settlers for 160 years (1770–1930) although they had only spears with which to fight. African slaves escaped slavery by running away, by rebellion, and even by committing suicide. The Maroons, a community of escaped slaves in Jamaica, carried out a successful guerrilla campaign against the white plantation owners for a hundred years. In India and Africa there were long periods of struggle for independence against the European colonial powers. These struggles often involved civil disobedience, strikes, and even armed combat.

In the late twentieth century, most of the former colonies of the Western powers won independence. Finally, in 1994, South Africa freed itself from

Kenya's demand for independence was finally granted by the British government in 1963. This picture shows the Duke of Edinburgh (left) and the first Kenyan president, Jomo Kenyatta, at the Independence Day ceremony.

apartheid. Despite these hard-won changes, racism and exploitation continue. The movement of people based on slavery and colonialism has been followed by the movement of people to the Western industrialized countries that needed workers. In these societies, ethnic minority groups continue to face discrimination and prejudice. When there have been problems like high unemployment or a shortage of housing, minority groups have often been blamed—although they were not the cause of the economic crisis. In societies where colonized peoples have gained their independence, creating an independent, free, equal, and successful society has been difficult. This is partly because the economy and institutions in their countries were developed to serve the interests of the former colonial rulers. This is true of countries such as India and, more recently, South Africa. Hence the struggle for equal rights remains an important political movement worldwide. This book looks at the problem of racism in several parts of the world and suggests how people, including young people, can play an important role in fighting racism.

One of the most influential nationalist leaders who compaigned for Indian independence was Mahatma Gandhi. He led a nonviolent campaign of civil disobedience against the British government. Here he is met by a crowd of his supporters as he arrives at Delhi station in 1935. India subsequently gained independence from the British in 1947.

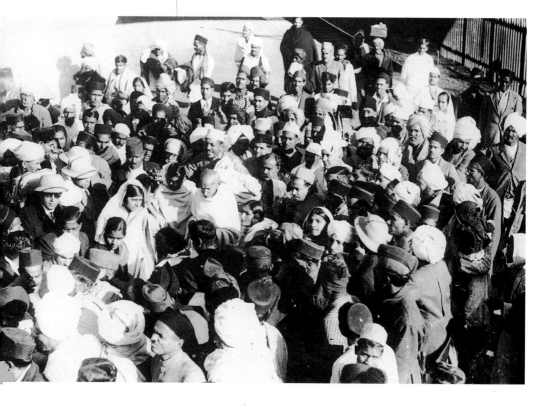

MIGRATION AND CITIZENSHIP —RACISM IN EUROPE

Asian women assemble electronic toys in a British factory.

Multiracial Europe

Although small numbers of black and ethnic minority people have lived in Europe for centuries, many more have come to live in Europe since World War II (1939–45). This pattern of migration resulted from the growth of industries, which continued to expand after the war ended. As a result, many industrial countries experienced a shortage of labor and looked outside their borders for workers. Some of these workers came from outside Europe, for example, from North Africa, South Asia, and the Caribbean. Others came from poorer parts of Europe such as Turkey, Spain, Yugoslavia, and southern Italy. Most of this migration took place in the 1950s and 1960s.

Bringing workers in from other countries was so important for the success of Europe's industry that, by the early 1970s, there were about 11 million migrant workers in Europe. About 14 percent of manual laborers in Germany and Great Britain were immigrants, as were a quarter of the industrial workforce in France, Belgium, and Switzerland.

66 99

•••

What Europe wanted, though, was the labour not the labourer...

Source:
A. Sivanandan, 1991

By this time, however, the European economies had begun to slow down. New technology reduced the number of workers necessary to do the same jobs. As unemployment rose and poverty grew, black and ethnic minorities were often blamed. Yet these people were often the first to lose their jobs. Some politicians were blaming migrants for problems that resulted from the failure of governments to prevent poverty and unemployment. For example, in 1980, the Dutch political party Centrum Partij used as its slogan: "500,000 foreigners in our country and 500,000 unemployed." During this period, governments started to introduce strict immigration control. Now only family members coming to join workers already living in a country and refugees escaping from persecution in their own countries can legally emigrate to Europe. Even these groups can find it very difficult to gain entry.

A nursing assistant in a hospital in London, England

Fact File

Black and ethnic minority populations in some European countries

Belgium
Total population: 9.9 million, of whom 85,000 are Turkish, 142,000 Moroccan, and 62,000 other Africans and Asians.

Denmark
Total population: 5.1 million, of whom 30,000 are Turkish, 7,000 African, and 38,000 Asian.

France
Total population: 56.5 million, of whom 198,000 are Turkish, 500,000 Moroccan, 614,000 Algerian, 206,000 Tunisian, 200,000 other African, and 227,000 Asian.

Germany
Total population: 79.7 million, of whom 1.7 million are Turkish, 198,000 African, and 500,000 Asian.

Italy
Total population: 57.7 million, of whom 238,000 are African and 140,000 Asian.

Great Britain
Total population: 56.7 million, of whom 29,000 are Turkish, 148,000 African, 72,000 Caribbean, and 453,000 Asian.

Note: The preceding figures only include people from ethnic minorities who are not already citizens of the various European countries.

Pakistani immigrants in Rome, Italy, earn a living by making candy.

Citizens of Europe?

Most European countries controlled immigration by operating a "guest worker" system, by which workers were invited to work in a country under fixed-term contracts. They were expected to leave the country when the contract was over. However, in Great Britain, migrants came as settlers rather than as "guest workers" because they were British subjects from the former colonies.

A store for Turkish guest workers in Munich, Germany

In most countries there are very strict rules for gaining citizenship, even when families have been born and brought up in that country. To become a citizen of Denmark, one must have lived there for seven years, speak perfect Danish, and owe no debts to the government. To become a citizen of Germany you must have lived permanently in the country for at least ten years and be at least eighteen years old. Other conditions to be met include having a knowledge of the German language, housing of an acceptable standard, a reliable income, and a willingness to adopt a German way of life. Some people do not think it is right that migrants to Germany should be asked to meet conditions like these—conditions that not all Germans are able to meet. Should ethnic minorities be expected to give up their culture and take on that of their adopted country? Europeans who migrate and live in other countries do not, as a rule, adopt the cultures of their new homes.

Living in racist Europe

Black and ethnic minorities continue to contribute a great deal to the European economy. In Germany, for example, "migrants," as a group, pay more in taxes than they receive in benefits. Despite this, ethnic minority communities face hostility and discrimination in their daily lives.

In many countries political support for right-wing political parties has increased alarmingly. Their supporters have campaigned against immigration and have been openly hostile to "foreigners." The economic recession of the 1970s is still not over, and most countries face problems of rising crime as well as economic hardship. In these circumstances, political parties of the right, who blame ethnic minorities for these problems, have begun to gain some support from the public.

Fact File

In Germany, 70 percent of the Turkish community are the children of Turkish immigrants and were born in Germany. Because of Germany's citizenship laws, they are still seen as foreigners and not as German citizens. The Turkish community has often been attacked by neo-Nazi groups. When the Turks fight back, they are threatened with deportation.

(Above) Thousands of people gather at the Pont du Carrousel in Paris, France, in May 1995. They are demonstrating against the action of skinheads, who had thrown a Moroccan youth to his death in the Seine River.

(Left) A youth aims a stone at police who attempt to control a violent anti-immigration riot in Rostock, Germany, in 1993. The violence was provoked by supporters of fascist, right-wing political parties in Germany.

Members of the right gain support by spreading racist ideas, which suggest that ethnic minorities are taking resources (for example, jobs, good housing, and hospital services) away from white people and are responsible for rising crime. For example, in Denmark in 1992, there were many newspaper stories blaming refugees from Yugoslavia for shoplifting and other petty crimes. In this climate, a Danish youth who bombed a refugee center said that his attack was to punish shoplifters.

Europe's ethnic minorities often meet racial discrimination in education, housing, employment, and other services. Often they face the threat of racial harassment and violence. In Holland, for example, the unemployment rate for ethnic minorities is two to three times that for the Dutch. Ethnic minorities do not have the same educational opportunities as whites, and even those who have similar educational qualifications find it harder to get skilled jobs than white people do. Many young people from ethnic minorities feel that they will never find regular work.

Ethnic minorities live mainly in the older, run-down districts of the larger cities—areas where housing and social services are poor. In Paris, a recent study found that 40 percent of lodgings without running water were occupied by families of foreign origin.

Racial harassment and violence

Economic conditions in Europe have been getting worse throughout the nineties. As a result, there are fewer jobs, decent houses, and other resources to go around. Governments have restricted immigration and the right to asylum for refugees and have therefore encouraged negative feelings about immigration. All this has encouraged a growing set of people to be hostile to ethnic minorities. People have been killed or violently attacked because of their race. Jewish cemeteries have been destroyed, racist graffiti scrawled on walls and doors, firebombs thrown into people's homes, and racist demonstrations held in the streets.

Ethnic minorities are often forced to live in run-down, inner-city areas such as Tower Hamlets in London, England.

Fact File

Racial harassment and violence in some European countries

Belgium

Antwerp, November 1992 Three Moroccans were attacked at a café.

Liege and Brussels, 1993 A number of racist killings took place.

Denmark

1992–93 Refugee asylum centers were bombed.

France

1992 At least eight North Africans died as a result of racist incidents.

Norway

1992 A number of terrorist attacks, including a neo-Nazi bombing of an "immigrant" school near Oslo, took place.

Switzerland

1992 Many attacks were carried out, including setting fire to buildings and bombing refugee centers. Two people died.

Turkish immigrants demonstrate against the firebombing of a Turkish home in Solingen, Germany, in 1993.

Paris policeman's crusade unmasks racism in uniform

Mr. Poiteaux was a recruit of seventeen days to the police force in Courbevoie on the outskirts of Paris when his superior told him, in March 1990, to issue a ticket to a car belonging to a local businessman of Tunisian origin, Alexandre Khelil.

Mr. Poiteaux refused on the grounds that the car was parked legally. His boss said he should not show so much sympathy for a "dirty Arab." She told him he should "systematically fine" all the Arab traders in the district.

The scene quickly degenerated into a showdown between the superior officer, Brigadier Marie-France Jubeault and the traders, many of whom came out in support of Mr. Poiteaux and Mr. Khelil.

"Get back to your own country, you don't make the rules around here," Brigadier Jubeault told the crowd growing around her.

Mr. Khelil received the maximum fine of $180 for parking in a bus lane, even though no bus lane exists outside his shop. In the next three months, he and his employees received a staggering 380 parking tickets for a total of some $121,000. Mr. Poiteaux was suspended from his job for insubordination....

Because of his suspension, Mr. Poiteaux was ineligible for unemployment benefits and had to live off the charity of friends, including Mr. Khelil, the welfare system and antiracist groups while he brought his case to court.

The first hearing, in 1992, went in his favor, but took another two years to be confirmed by the council of the state, the highest appeal court....The strain of these victories was enormous ....

Arsonists set fire to Mr. Poiteaux's apartment on two occasions, apparently to intimidate him. He was arrested on suspicion of armed robbery and held in custody for 48 hours before being released. He was also burgled, although the thieves left his television and VCR, taking only documents relating to the case.

"I've lived in fear all this time, and I'm still afraid," Mr. Poiteaux said. "I'm obviously an embarrassment to the police because I stumbled upon something they would rather no one knew about."

Source: *Guardian*, November 1994

Fighting racism

Large numbers of Europeans have been horrified by the evidence of the rise of racism, and many have actively fought against it. These individuals have been from colleges, trade unions, anti-racist groups, and black and ethnic minority groups.

Following large-scale racist attacks on refugees and other immigrants in 1992–93, many German people demonstrated by forming "candle chains" in Berlin, Munich, Frankfurt, and Hamburg. In Frankfurt 5,000 school students marched against the activities of the neo-Nazis. In 1994, in Britain, trade unions organized a 50,000-strong march against racism in the East End of London where a fascist councillor had been elected. All across Europe, many other activities, including rock concerts, poster campaigns, and advertising campaigns on television, have been organized to protest against racism.

Children pose in front of posters that advertise a Trades Union Congress march against racism in London.

A demonstration against homelessness, racism, and unemployment in Paris, in 1995

SOUTH AFRICA AND THE VICTORY OVER APARTHEID

How apartheid developed

Before Europeans arrived in South Africa, there was already a complex society of many African peoples with different languages and traditions. These included Bantu-speaking peoples, the Nguni, the Thonga, the Hottentots, and the San. In 1652, the Dutch established a port of call at the Cape of Good Hope on the tip of South Africa for taking on fresh provisions on the important sea route between Europe and the East. A small colony grew up around it. During this period, most of the Hottentot and San peoples who lived there were killed so that the Dutch settlers could take their land. Many of those who survived were taken as slaves. Slaves were also brought from the Dutch East Indies (modern-day Indonesia) to work for the settlers. In 1815, the British took control of the Cape Colony.

A Boer family on the move. Notice that they have taken their black slave with them.

A British army regiment in camp during the Boer War in 1900

At this time, there was conflict between the Dutch farmers (Boers) and the British, particularly when the British abolished slavery. The Dutch relied on slaves to run their farms. As a result, the Dutch started moving inland, waging wars with the African peoples of the interior. Between 1867 and 1886, diamonds and gold were discovered in inland areas of South Africa, and this led the British to wish to control the interior. There were wars between the British and the Dutch (the Boer Wars, 1880–1881 and 1899–1902) and with the Zulus, the most powerful of the African peoples. The African peoples were defeated by the superior military strength of the Europeans and particularly by their firearms, which the Africans did not have.

In 1910, the British government passed the Act of Union, which united the Boer and British colonies of South Africa under one government. Later, in 1926, the Union of South Africa declared its independence from Great Britain. By the time of the Union, there were already laws in the Boer and British colonies that forced many blacks to work on white-owned farms and in white-owned mines for low wages and denied them any social and political rights. For example, blacks did not have the right to vote and were only allowed to live in certain areas. The Union made it possible to extend this system throughout South Africa. In 1948 the National Party won an election, with apartheid (meaning "apartness") as its official policy.

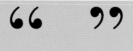

• • •

White people in South Africa justified their treatment of black people with racist ideas of white superiority.

Apartheid is a way of saving the white civilization from vanishing beneath the black sea of South Africa's non-European populations.

Source: Dr. D. F. Malan, Leader of the National Party, 1948

The National Party was strongly supported by the Dutch Reformed Church.

God divided humanity into races, languages and nations. Differences are not only willed by God, but perpetuated by Him.... Those who are culturally and spiritually advanced have a mission to leadership and protection of the less advanced.

Source: Commission of the Dutch Reformed Church, 1950

A black family, with their possessions, is being resettled in the black homeland of KwaZulu.

Apartheid in practice

Apartheid meant that all South Africa's people were officially classified into whites, coloreds (mixed race and Asians), and natives (blacks). Mixed marriages between different so-called races were made illegal. The Group Areas Act of 1950 set up separate areas for racial groups to live in; for example, black townships outside major cities and black "homelands" in rural areas. In 1953, an act was passed making it an offense for blacks to mix with whites on trains and buses, in swimming pools, on beaches, and even on park benches.

Not only did apartheid separate people, it also kept people unequal. For example, in the townships black people had poor housing, poor schools, and poor medical services. In the white areas, people enjoyed a high standard of living. Black South Africans were forced to work for white employers because there were few jobs in the "homelands." This often meant having to travel long distances and living away from home.

A bridge for "whites only" at a train station in Johannesburg, South Africa, in 1980

This brief history shows how white settlers used their military strength to defeat and dominate the African peoples in order to control the land and mineral wealth of South Africa. In this way, a white minority was able to establish control over a black majority. In 1995, there were 22.5 million black people living in South Africa—74 percent of the population.

These schoolchildren from Cape Town, South Africa, carry placards protesting against apartheid at an antiapartheid demonstration.

Fact File

Young people have been an important part of the struggle against apartheid, with strikes and boycotts led by school students. In 1976, students from Soweto, a black township, took part in a demonstration against the inferior education provided for blacks. The police opened fire on the unarmed demonstration and 176 people, mainly children and young people, were killed. Since 1976, nearly 1,000 black children have been killed by police bullets.

66 99 ...

There was a girl
eight years old, they say
her hair in spiky braids
her innocent fist raised in imitation

Afterwards, there was a mass of red
some torn pieces of meat
and bright rags fluttering:
a girl in a print dress, once, they say.

Source: Dennis Brutus

Opposition to apartheid

From the early wars against the white settlers to the more recent political and armed struggles against apartheid, black South Africans have fought against their unjust treatment at the hands of Europeans. These struggles have included industrial strikes against white employers, public demonstrations, campaigns for equal rights, and guerrilla war waged from neighboring black African states.

Students from Johannesburg University demonstrate for the release of Nelson Mandela in 1987.

Throughout the history of apartheid, the South African police and army brutally put down all forms of resistance. Often people who protested were imprisoned and even murdered.

Many organizations were formed to oppose apartheid, including the Pan Africanist Congress and the Inkatha Freedom party. One of the most important organizations formed to fight apartheid was the African National Congress (ANC). In the 1940s, a number of young people, including Nelson Mandela, Oliver Tambo, and Walter Sisulu, formed the Youth League of the ANC. This group helped organize protests against apartheid. In 1962, Nelson Mandela was arrested and imprisoned on minor charges and then tried again for treason in 1963–64. At his trial in 1964, Nelson Mandela gave a famous speech. He said:

During my lifetime I have dedicated myself to this struggle of the African people. I have fought against white domination and I have fought against black domination. I have cherished the idea of a democratic and free society in which all persons live together in harmony and with equal opportunities. It is an ideal which I hope to live for and achieve. But if needs be, it is an ideal for which I am prepared to die.

Nelson Mandela (right)—
the first black president of
South Africa

As the struggle against apartheid became fierce, and the brutality of the South African army and police became clear for all to see, other countries were forced by public opinion to take action. Some countries refused to trade with South Africa and refused, for example, to compete with South African players in international sports. International pressure was put on the South African government for the release of Nelson Mandela and the abolition of apartheid. This included demonstrations outside the South African Embassy and a huge "Free Nelson Mandela" concert in London in 1989. Businessmen in South Africa began to argue for change. They could see that their success was being threatened by international companies' refusal to invest in South Africa.

The release of Nelson Mandela

In February 1990, after nearly thirty years, Nelson Mandela was released from prison amidst much rejoicing across the world. The tide had truly turned. President F. W. De Klerk, who had become the leader of the National Party in 1989, told his white parliament "the time for negotiation has arrived." He could see that the future of South Africa must lie in getting rid of apartheid. Slowly he began to take steps to dismantle aspects of apartheid and to negotiate with the ANC toward the most fundamental change of all: one person, one vote.

The election

The first free elections in South Africa, in which all adults were able to take part, took place between April 26–29, 1994. Black people taking part had never had the chance to vote before. Before the election, the ANC had worked hard to educate people on the importance of the election and how to exercise their voting rights. At the election, there were lines of up to two miles long at many polling stations, and people waited for up to eight hours in the sun to vote.

Fact File

Election results

African National Congress (62.6 percent of the vote)	252 seats
National Party	82 seats
Inkatha (Zulu party)	43 seats
Other parties	23 seats
Total	400 seats

Blacks and whites line up to vote in South Africa's first nonracial elections in 1994.

Rebuilding South Africa

The ANC's election manifesto and program, *The Reconstruction and Development Programme,* set out its plans for rebuilding South Africa. It points out that South Africa today, as a result of the racism of apartheid, faces many problems.

• Poverty and misery exist alongside modern conveniences and wealth.

• A majority of black people have suffered from poor education and training and are economically deprived.

• A minority of whites control a large part of the economy, and skills are concentrated in white hands.

• The violence of apartheid has created a culture of violence, and people feel unsafe.

Black poverty in a South African squatter camp in Cape Town

A black family home in a township in South Africa

As a result of the struggle against apartheid, South Africa also has an enormous strength: the collective determination to build a new South Africa. There are many problems to solve. Look at the Fact File to the right and decide, if you were a member of the ANC, how you would tackle the problems.

The challenge ahead

It has taken over 250 years for black South Africans to regain their freedom. This struggle will need to continue if South Africans, black and white, are to build a free and equal South Africa. The constitution in the new South Africa does not divide people on the grounds of race. However, this does not mean that the division has disappeared.

Fact File

The key programs of *The Reconstruction and Development Programme* of the African National Congress in 1994

Meeting basic needs
- redistribute a substantial amount of land to landless people
- build over one million houses
- provide clean water and sanitation for all
- bring electricity to 2.5 million homes
- provide affordable health care and telecommunications

Developing human resources
- provide education and training for all, especially for young people
- ensure an equal role for women
- restructure industry to reenter the world economy
- develop an arts and culture program that recognizes cultural diversity
- provide sports and recreational facilities for all

Building the economy
- establish trade unions and workers' rights
- cooperate with neighboring African countries
- give equal access to jobs and training to all

Democratizing the state and society
- develop local government
- reform police and security forces
- establish a bill of rights

After his first year as president, Mandela warned the South African people that it would be a long and difficult task to deliver the government's promises. There are not only the huge problems of building decent houses and schools and creating worthwhile jobs for millions of black people that have to be solved. The bitter memories, the prejudices, and the mistrust of the people toward a national reconciliation will also have to be overcome.

(Right) Victory over apartheid at last. Crowds celebrate Mandela's success after the 1994 election.

(Below right) Two people in the crowd listen to Mandela's first speech as president of South Africa.

Media Watch

Black day for white police

Traffic officer A.9 C. du Preez was only doing what came naturally. He was riding his motorcycle down a busy Pretoria thoroughfare on a Saturday night when he spotted a car double-parked outside a Kentucky Fried Chicken fast-food restaurant.

Officer du Preez stopped and shouted to the black driver of the parked vehicle: "Remove the bloody car!" This being the new South Africa, the black man complained that there was no need for such rude behavior whereupon Officer du Preez warned him not to answer back. "Who do you think you are? I'll hit you!" he said.

The black man continued to remonstrate [argue], which left the traffic officer—an Afrikaner evidently still trapped in the old apartheid ways—with no option but to grab the driver by the throat and pack him off to the police station.

It was only after he had been holding the man at the precinct for 20 minutes that Officer du Preez made an appalling discovery: his victim was none other then Sydney Mufamadi, the Minister of Police....

Mr. Mufamadi, a former trade unionist, is a youthful-looking 37 whose favored mode of off-duty dress is blue jeans and black leather jacket. Officer du Preez, despite having taken possession of Mr. Mufamadi's passport with all his ministerial particulars, proved incapable of reconciling himself to the idea that a man this color, this young and of this demeanor [appearance] could possibly be who he said he was.

Officer du Preez will no doubt be spending the foreseeable future bent double in an attitude of abject despair. As for his immediate boss, the Pretoria traffic chief, Tienie van Rensburg, he volunteered the comforting thought that the lesson to be drawn from the incident is that the law treated everybody equally.

Source: *Independent*, November 1994

66 99
...

If people don't want to forgive, there is no way that we are going to have a new beginning.
Source: Archbishop Desmond Tutu, October 1994

RACISM IN THE UNITED STATES

Racism in the Americas

In 1492, Christopher Columbus, an Italian explorer in the service of Spain, landed in the Caribbean. He had been trying to find a western sea route to India, so he called the islands he found the West Indies. Soon after, other seafarers from Spain explored South and Central America and found the gold and silver that were there.

Columbus and the Spanish did not discover the Americas. These countries were already inhabited by indigenous peoples such as the Caribs and Arawaks and included highly developed civilizations—for example, the Aztecs in Mexico and the Incas in Peru. The Spanish and later the Portuguese set about conquering the Americas by robbing and murdering not just individuals but whole peoples. In 150 years, the population of Aztecs, Incas, and Mayas was reduced from 80 million to about 3.5 million. The Spaniards held racist views that the indigenous peoples were barbaric and uncivilized, and so they justified their brutal treatment to themselves.

The Spanish and Portuguese began to settle in the Americas. They mined silver and started farms, using indigenous people as slaves for labor. Many died, so the Europeans began to import people from Africa to work in their place. The Americas became vital for European industry and trade as a source of food and raw materials, in particular sugar, cotton, and tobacco.

Of gold is treasure made, and with it he who has it does as he wills in the world and it even sends souls to Paradise.

Source: Christopher Columbus

Native American slaves, watched over by their Spanish overseer, prepare ore for a smelting works in Mexico.

The influence of the Spanish and the Portuguese on South and Central America has been very great. The very name Latin America and the mixture of peoples is a result of this influence.

North America
British settlers first landed in North America in 1620, when a small group of religious refugees founded the colony of Plymouth, Massachusetts. North America was already populated by indigenous peoples. The white settlers waged war on the Native Americans and stole their lands. Many of these people were killed. Native Americans today continue to fight legal battles to win compensation for lands that were stolen from them and to try to hold on to the land in their reservations.

A new European settlement in California in 1860

In 1783, the United States gained its independence by defeating the British armies. During the nineteenth century, huge plantations were created in the southern states to grow tobacco, rice, and cotton; people from Africa were enslaved as laborers. In the northern states, the number of factories began to grow. This led to an enormous demand for workers. Some of these workers came from Europe, but the factory owners also wanted to be able to employ people who were slaves from the south. The Civil War and the abolition of slavery meant that, as slaves were freed, they could become paid workers.

Slaves picking cotton on a plantation in Georgia in 1895

Between 1831 and 1920, over 30 million immigrants—90 percent from Europe—arrived in the United States to work in the growing industries. Recently, fewer immigrants have arrived from Europe and more from Asia and South and Central America. Since 1970, most immigrants have come from Mexico, the Philippines, Korea, Vietnam, Cuba, China, and India.

The struggle for civil rights

The ending of slavery did not bring equality to African-Americans. In the south, plantation owners were forced to employ their former slaves, but they refused to treat them as equals and paid low wages. The southern states passed laws to deny black people the right to vote and to keep them separate from white people. Racist groups such as the Ku Klux Klan were organized. Their members committed terrible crimes against black people, including murder. Even in the north, where many black people lived, they were treated badly and got the worst jobs, the worst housing, and the worst schools.

Throughout the history of slavery—and since—black people in the United States have fought for equal rights. For example, slaves escaped, rebelled, and organized revolts. Black people in the northern cities were involved in uprisings to protest against their bad living conditions. Black organizations were formed to campaign for equal rights. Their supporters led marches, organized demonstrations, and drew up petitions for better treatment. Throughout the 1960s, black leaders increased their demands for equality and civil rights. Some of these leaders were murdered in the struggle, including Martin Luther King, Jr. and Malcolm X.

A burning cross, a symbol of the Ku Klux Klan, towers over a recent meeting of the Klan.

" "

• • •

You don't catch hell because you're a Baptist, and you don't catch hell because you're a Methodist... you don't catch hell because you're a Democrat or Republican. You catch hell because you're a black man. You catch hell, all of us catch hell, for the same reason...we're all black people, so-called Negroes, second-class citizens, ex-slaves.

Source: Extract from a speech by Malcolm X, 1965

Hispanics and Asian-Americans have joined African- and Native Americans in the campaign for equal rights. As a result of the civil rights movement, some new laws have been passed and special programs developed to give a fairer deal to black people. Despite all of these struggles, the position of blacks and ethnic minorities in the United States is still unequal.

"Race" and racism in the United States today
Black Americans

In recent years the position of black Americans appears to have changed greatly. In 1984, Jesse Jackson was considered as a candidate for the presidential election. There has been a black Miss America and a black American in space. Today there are a number of black mayors in American cities, successful black businessmen, and famous black movie stars and athletes.

This march in 1983 in Washington, D.C., was held to commemorate the twentieth anniversary of Martin Luther King's 1963 civil rights march. The demand was still for "Jobs, Peace and Freedom."

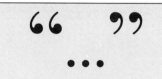

> 66　99
>
> • • •
>
> *We are in a situation more dangerous than slavery. We are becoming polarized again, so there is a middle class, and a professional class and a working class, an underclass, a literate class, a drug class and an illiterate class. We have almost a steel floor between the middle and the underclasses, so strong that only a few can puncture it.*
>
> Source: Maya Angelou, an African-American writer, 1989

However, while a few black Americans have become successful, there has also been a growth in the number of extremely poor black Americans—living in poor housing, with high levels of unemployment, and with poor education. This group is found mainly in America's larger industrial cities. Experts believe that the high levels of black poverty are the result of lingering racism and unequal treatment of black people, and because of the effects of the unequal treatment they received in the past.

For the last 30 years, the unemployment rate for black workers has been at least double that of the rest of the population. In 1994, 12 percent of black workers were unemployed, compared with 5 percent of whites. The position of young black workers is even worse. Among black teenagers looking for work, 44 percent were unemployed, compared with 17 percent among white teenagers.

Jesse Jackson, a prominent American politician

Figures from the early 1990s show that nearly one in three black families lives in poverty, compared with one in ten of the general population. In 1993, the average weekly earnings for black workers was $370 as compared with $478 for whites.

Hispanics
Hispanics make up approximately 8 percent of the U.S. population. Most of these people have lived in America for several generations, but they are still seen as an immigrant minority. The main groups are Mexican Americans, Hispanics from Central and South America, Puerto Ricans, and Cubans.

One in four Hispanic families lives in poverty. The average earnings for some groups of Hispanic workers is even lower than that of black workers. The average weekly earnings of Puerto Ricans in 1987 was $292. Unemployment for Hispanics in 1990 was 7.7 percent, one-and-a-half times that of the white population. Only 55 percent of Hispanic workers have full-time, year-round jobs. Part of the cause of unemployment and poverty in the Hispanic community is widespread racial discrimination in the job market. As a result of poverty, 40 percent of Hispanic youths drop out of high school. A teenager's salary is often needed to pay the rent or put food on the table.

A large proportion of the population in New York City is of Hispanic origin.

Asian-Americans
Asian-Americans make up about 4 percent of the population. Most are American-born descendants of immigrants from China, Japan, Korea, India, the Philippines, or the Pacific Islands. Some are recent immigrants from these countries or from Vietnam, Cambodia, and Laos.

Asian-Americans face widespread racial prejudice and discrimination. Many European Americans think people of Asian origin are foreigners, even when their families have been American citizens for generations. Some Americans even blame Asian-Americans for economic problems resulting from economic competition from Japan, Korea, and other Asian countries. There has been racist violence against Asians across the United States, as there is against other minority groups.

Fact File

The effects of poverty, unemployment, and racism have been to make black and other minorities, understandably, feel angry and discontented, and this has created tensions within the communities where they live. White people who are poor and unemployed can also feel frustrated. These tensions can boil over and lead to disturbances in which people show their discontent. Sometimes these disturbances become violent.

Events in Los Angeles (see the Fact File) have shown America that antidiscrimination laws and programs have only benefited a few black Americans and other minorities. For most, Martin Luther King, Jr.'s dream of equality is as far away as ever. In a famous speech made in 1963, he said:

I have a dream my four little children will one day live in a nation where they will not be judged by the color of their skin but by the content of their character. I have a dream today…

A row of burned-out buildings still smolders days after the 1992 Los Angeles riots.

INDIGENOUS PEOPLES— RACISM IN AUSTRALIA

European settlement in Australia

Today the "typical" Australian is white, having descended from European—mostly English and Irish—settlers. But the first Australians were the Aborigines, and they are regaining a foothold in Australian society. As in Africa and the Americas, European settlers occupied Australia [and New Zealand] and destroyed many of the indigenous people. In this chapter, we look at the position of Aboriginal peoples in Australia today.

Aboriginal peoples estimate that they have lived on the Australian continent for 50,000 years. Scattered around the country were some 500 Aboriginal societies and groups. The people lived as hunters and gatherers, never taking more than they needed. Their way of life was based on preserving the land and its resources and not damaging them. There was no need to develop complex technology. In most places there was enough food to meet the needs of the people. Cooperation and sharing were important values, with everybody helping to support the whole group. These peoples developed a complex culture that included their own languages, religions, art, and traditions.

The first recorded contact between Europeans and the Aboriginal peoples was in 1606 when a Dutch ship landed at Mapoon in northern Queensland. The indigenous people successfully drove

Aboriginal peoples lived in harmony with the land.

The home of a white settler family in the Australian bush in 1899

them away. In 1770, British seaman Captain Cook landed in Australia to take possession of the country for England. In 1788, the British began to send convicts from overcrowded British prisons to Australia. This was followed by further large-scale British migration. People came in search of gold and other minerals and to set up farming communities. The year 1788 is usually seen as the beginning of the European settlement of Australia.

The Aboriginal peoples fought hard to keep their lands. However, they were eventually overpowered by the superior weapons of the Europeans. The Europeans brought with them racist ideas about non-European people. They thought the Aboriginal people were primitive, almost like animals. These ideas helped them to justify in their minds the taking of the lands from Aboriginal groups. Over the next 150 years, 80 percent of the Aboriginal population was killed in wars, massacres, and by diseases caught from the Europeans. Survivors were allowed to settle on reserves, controlled by the white authorities, and were used as cheap labor.

Fact File

Australian population by origin

- *Australia (Indigenous Aboriginal peoples)* 250,000 (1.6%)

- *Vietnam* 119,000 (0.8%)

- *Lebanon* 68,000 (0.5%)

- *Philippines* 62,000 (0.5%)

- *India* 55,000 (0.45%)

- *Malaysia* 54,000 (0.45%)

- *Hong Kong and China* 92,000 (0.75%)

- *Europe (largely Britain and Ireland)* 16.3 million (95%)

Australia today

Of the 17 million people living in Australia today, some 1.6 percent are indigenous peoples (approximately a quarter of a million). The majority of the European people are of British and Irish descent. Until 1973, no immigration was allowed from non-European countries. Since that time, immigrants to Australia have been more likely to be of Asian origin than European. Of the Australian population, 22 percent were born overseas; approximately 40 percent have either arrived since 1947 or are the children of these migrants.

Racism and discrimination

Aboriginal peoples were nearly wiped out during the period of European settlement. As recently as the 1960s, many Aboriginal children were forcibly removed from their mothers to be raised as whites and to be trained as manual or domestic labor for white employers. This happened especially to children of Aboriginal mothers and white fathers.

Aborigines at the opening of a Pacific arts festival with Australian government mininster Charles Perkins, who is himself an Aboriginal

This song was written by an Aborigine who as a little boy was taken away from his mother.

Yowie, yowie, my brown skin baby
They take him away.
Between her sobs I heard her say
Police 'bin take my baby away,
From white man boss baby I had,
Why he let them take baby away?

To a children's home the baby came
With new clothes on and a new name,
But day and night he would always say,
Mummy, oh mummy why they take me away,
Yowie, yowie, my brown skin baby
They take him away.

—Bob Randall

A cave painting in Arnhem Land, Northern Territory. Aboriginal peoples have lived in Australia for 50,000 years and have a distinctive and rich culture of their own.

A family in Redfern, a mainly Aborignal area of Sydney, Australia

It was not until 1967 that the Aboriginal people were granted full citizenship rights; for example, the right to vote and to own land. Even though the Aboriginal people now have the same rights as other Australians, in practice they continue to suffer discrimination. They remain a very poor section of Australian society. Rates of unemployment, infant deaths, and disease are much higher among the Aboriginal people than among the rest of the population. For example, the average life expectancy of an Aboriginal person is twenty years less than other Australians. In Sydney, which has good health care facilities, 25 percent of Aboriginal children are seriously malnourished. Official reports show that the Aboriginal people suffer the worst discrimination of any group in Australia. Evidence produced in the early 1990s showed cases of ill-treatment of Aboriginal people by the police, including unwarranted shootings, brutality, beatings, and false arrests.

Media Watch

Police crossword racist

A racist crossword, displayed in a South Australian police station, has sparked fresh allegations about racism in the police forces.

The director of the Aboriginal Legal Rights movement of South Australia, Sandra Saunders, said last night that the crossword was displayed on an internal door of a country police station last July. After a complaint was made, a police officer admitted authorship, and $125 was deducted from his pay for a breach of discipline.

Among the racist "clues" and answers on the crossword were:
• The locals we would all like to exterminate. (*Answer*: niggers.)
• Niggers, unlike dogs, cannot be taught these as they are too stupid. (*Answer*: tricks.)
• If the niggers all did this the town would be great. (*Answer*: go.)
• Where niggers are involved you should always___to kill. (*Answer*: shoot.)

A spokesman for the South Australian police, Senior Sergeant Mick Symonds, said last night, "The matter has been dealt with by the Police Complaints Authority. It's all over and done with. There's no comment to be made."

The officer remains on the police force.

Saunders said the crossword was a "very clear example of the grossest form of racism."

Source: the Australian newspaper *The Age*, March, 1992

Racial harassment, including intimidation and violence, against Aboriginal and other visible ethnic minorities has also taken place. This has included attacks on refugees from Vietnam and Cambodia. In 1989, a national inquiry by the Australian government found evidence of small neo-Nazi groups involved in racist violence.

An Aboriginal woman at a land rights protest

"We have survived"— Aboriginal struggles against racism

A common slogan among Aborigines today is "We have survived." Aboriginal struggles against racism and injustice, which started with wars against the first European immigrants, have continued. In 1972, Aborigines set up a "Tent Embassy" in the federal capital, Canberra, to demand equal rights, including respect for their culture and freedom from racism. In particular they asked for the land rights of Aborigines, as the original and legal owners of Australia, to be recognized. Aboriginal groups in some areas have been given back some of their original land. This could change in the future because of the discovery of rich mineral deposits that the government wishes to use. Aborigines have begun to organize their own health services, schools, housing associations, and radio stations. Books have been published by Aboriginal poets, playwrights, and historians. Art, dance, and music from Aboriginal culture have gained international recognition.

Aborigines protesting against the 1988 bicentennial celebrations

I am of the earth.
I am a son of the earth.
I am the trees, the rivers, the rock,
I am kin to the earth's creatures,
I am kin to the earth's creations.
The earth is my mother.

The white man is also of the earth.
But he is mad,
For what man in his right mind
Would rape his own mother.

—Wandjuk Marika, Aboriginal poet, 1977

The 1988 Australian Bicentennial: "Nothing to celebrate"

In January 1988, in Sydney, white Australians celebrated the 200th anniversary of modern Australia. This included a huge carnival with ships, fireworks, and parties on the beach. The British royal family joined the event.

In Central Park, Sydney, ten thousand Aborigines, young and old, held a mourning for what they called 200 years of land theft and murder: "Nothing to celebrate." Later the march changed to a celebration: "We have survived."

An important part of the struggle for equal rights has been to regain pride in being an Aborigine. This had been denied by the racist views of European settlers.

Gold medalist Cathy Freeman carries the Aboriginal flag in the lap after winning her race at the Commonwealth Games in 1994.

A good example of the pride of modern Aborigines can be found in the picture on the left. At the 1994 Commonwealth Games in Victoria, Australia, an Aboriginal athlete, Cathy Freeman, won the 400-meter event. On her victory lap she insisted on carrying the Aboriginal flag instead of the Australian flag, despite the protests of some officials.

ALL DIFFERENT—ALL EQUAL

Racism has shaped our world historically and continues to affect people's lives today. Racism damages us all. Racism affects those who are at the receiving end of racist violence and discrimination; it also affects those who think that they are superior to other people, and that it is all right to treat others badly. All of us, black and white, male and female, young and old, ethnic minorities and majorities, suffer when we are forced to live in a society of hatred. All of us would be safer, freer, and happier if we lived in a society in which all people are treated equally and fairly. Pastor Martin Niemöller, a victim of the Nazis in World War II, wrote:

First they came for the Jews
and I did not speak out—
because I was not a Jew.

Then they came for the Communists
and I did not speak out—
because I was not a Communist.

Then they came for the trade unionists
and I did not speak out—
because I was not a trade unionist.

Then they came for me—
and there was no one left
to speak out for me.

People have always fought against racism. Some people have lost their lives in the struggle against racism. Black and ethnic minority people have often led the way in this fight but white people, too, have had an important part to play in making the world closer to equal. In this chapter, we will be looking at ways in which we can all help in this struggle.

American civil rights leader, Martin Luther King, Jr., who was assassinated in 1968

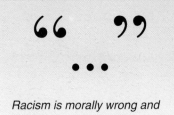

Racism is morally wrong and politically dangerous. It concerns us all. For if we divide our people by sex, by race or by nation, we all lose.

Source: *Declaration on Racial Violence and Xenophobia*, signed by European Socialist Leaders, June 1993

Fact File

On November 9, 1994, people from thirty European countries took part in protests against the racist treatment of Gypsies in much of Europe. Gypsy sites and homes were being attacked, and the Gypsies were receiving little protection from police and limited rights to health and social welfare. Action against this treatment of Gypsies included writing letters and postcards to the embassies of countries where this was taking place. Demonstrations also took place in Amsterdam, Bonn, Budapest, Copenhagen, Helsinki, Madrid, Moscow, and Paris. The date November 9 was chosen because it marks the anniversary of *Kristallnacht* in Germany, when the windows of Jewish stores, homes, and synagogues were smashed. That night, in 1938, marked a new stage in the persecution of the Jews, which was to culminate in the Holocaust, when six million people were killed in concentration camps. Among these victims, who were mainly Jews, were half a million Gypsies.

After the overthrow of the Communist government in 1989, racial abuse of the Gypsies in Czechoslovakia steadily increased. In this picture, demonstrators, headed by leaders from three Gypsy pressure groups, march to Prague Castle to protest racial violence.

Human rights

After World War II had ended, the murder of millions of Jews (as well as Gypsies, homosexuals, and others) came to light. Many people thought that there should be a worldwide organization to help to prevent war in the future and to promote human rights for all the peoples of the world. As a result, the United Nations was formed. In 1948, forty-eight countries signed the Universal Declaration of Human Rights. This declaration sets out the way in which countries, governments, and people should behave toward one another and the basic rights that all people should have.

There are two groups of rights contained in the declaration. One group is concerned with our economic, social, and cultural rights. These include the right to food and shelter, the right to health and education, the right to work and to choose one's work freely, the right to earn equal pay for equal work, and the right to leisure and to artistic and cultural activity. The second group of rights is our civil and political rights. These include our right to life, to liberty, and to security, the right to a fair trial, the right to choose one's government, the right to travel freely, and the right to express our ideas and opinions freely. The declaration makes it clear that these rights should be for everyone.

In May 1945, after the ending of World War II in Europe, leaders of the five big powers—the U.S., Great Britain, France, Russia, and China met to discuss a United Nations Charter.

Eleanor Roosevelt, wife of a former United States President, standing second from left, presents a guidebook on the Universal Declaration of Human Rights to the United Nations. This ceremony, which took place at United Nations Headquarters in New York City, was part of the 1958 worldwide celebrations of the tenth anniversary of the signing of this document.

Fact File

The United Nations Universal Declaration of Human Rights 1948

Article 1
All human beings are born free and equal in dignity and rights. They are endowed with reason and conscience and should act towards one another in a spirit of brotherhood.

Article 2
Everyone is entitled to all the rights and freedoms set forth in this Declaration, without distinction of any kind, such as race, colour, sex, language, political or other opinion, national or social origin, property, birth or other status.

Article 7
All are equal before the law and are entitled without any discrimination to equal protection of the law. All are entitled to equal protection against any discrimination in violation of this Declaration and against any incitement to such discrimination.

The United Nations Children's Fund (UNICEF) has been working to improve children's lives since 1946, when it was set up by the United Nations. UNICEF's work includes helping to promote and implement the United Nations Convention on the Rights of the Child.

Here, a UNICEF truck is collecting unaccompanied refugee children from Goma, a camp in Zaire, so that they can be given food and medical attention and, if possible, be reunited with their parents.

The declaration is not law and it is up to individual countries to put it into practice. The United Nations cannot force countries to respect the articles of the declaration. Since the declaration was passed, the United Nations has developed further agreements that hold governments more firmly to promises about people's rights. One example is the 1989 United Nations Convention on the Rights of the Child.

Even though nearly every country says it accepts the United Nations Universal Declaration on Human Rights, many people around the world do not have these rights. For example, racism around the world still promotes inequality, rather than equality, among people. It is up to all of us, individually and together, to try to make the idea of equal rights a reality for everyone.

What we can do

One of the things we can do is to challenge racism in our daily lives. Here are a few ideas.

• Never make jokes or insults about people's "race," culture, or the color of their skin

• Try to point out the false logic in racist comments and actions.

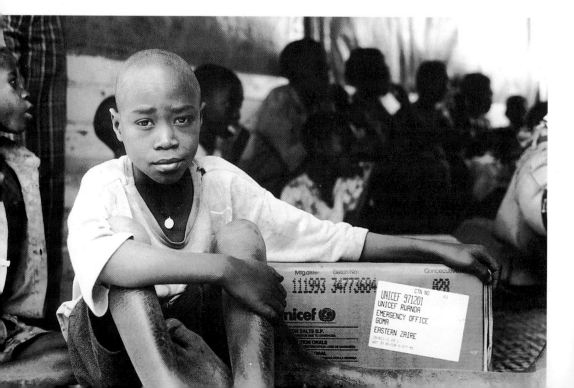

• Learn more about racism to understand how it affects everyone—and to be able to recognize even subtle forms of it.

• Talk to other students about racism in and work together to stop it.

A primary school playground, in 1990, in London, England. The pupils playing together are from many different ethnic backgrounds.

Fact File

United Nations Convention on the Rights of the Child, 1989

Article 30
In those states in which ethnic, religious or linguistic minorities or persons of indigenous origin exist, a child belonging to such a minority or who is indigenous shall not be denied the right, in common with other members of his or her group, to enjoy his or her culture, to profess and practise his or her own religion, or to use his or her own language.

Fact File

In many schools young people and their teachers have written policies about racism and how to prevent it. In one school in England, pupils and teachers wrote a *Respect for All* statement:

At Townsend School, we believe that every person is equally important and that no one has a right to harass, insult or cause offence to any other person for any reason.

We particularly reject the way that some people abuse others

• *because they are richer or poorer, older or younger*

• *because they are small or tall, thin or fat*

• *because of the color of their skin*

• *because they are male or female*

• *because they are a teacher or pupil*

• *because of their religion*

• *because of disability or personal problems*

• *because of their looks or what they wear*

• *because of their likes or dislikes*

• *because they are popular or unpopular*

• *because of their ability or lack of ability*

• *because of nationality or accent.*

We are all individuals with differences, but we are all members of Townsend and can learn from each other.

Protesters march in Paris, France, to voice opposition to racism and fascism, in May 1990.

We can also take part in organizations and events in our areas that are about human rights and that challenge racism and intolerance. One example of such events was the Rock Against Hate concerts organized in Switzerland in 1994. These included rock musicians from all over the world. This kind of event allows us to enjoy ourselves while we play a part in educating against racism.

Fact File

The Vikings of ancient Norway provided the inspiration for action against racism. The Viking people believed in two worlds: Asgard, the home of the gods; and Midgard, where human beings lived. According to legend, everyone could be equal in Midgard, where the color of the skin had no importance. This is why "Circus Midgard" was chosen as the name of a rock music tour that visited twenty-eight towns in Norway during 1994 as part of a national youth campaign against racism. The young people of Norway also questioned their country's leaders and demanded that a charter against racism be written. This charter included demands for action against racism.

Racism remains a serious problem in the world. There have been important victories against racism, for example, in the changes that have taken place in South Africa. At the same time, the conditions of many black and ethnic minority people remain unequal and unjust. International bodies like the United Nations cannot solve problems like this without the support of individuals. It is up to all of us to make sure that the future brings greater equality and justice to all of humankind.

A march against racial attacks in London, England

GLOSSARY

apartheid Literally "apartness;" the system introduced in 1948 by the white government of South Africa. It was designed to keep white, black, and colored peoples separate and unequal.

asylum The right to live in a country other than one's own. Refugees who are persecuted in their own countries, perhaps because of their "race," religion, or political beliefs, often flee to other countries to claim this right to protection.

citizen A person who has full rights within a particular country, including the right to live there permanently and to vote.

civil rights The rights of a citizen to political, racial, legal, and social freedom or equality.

colonialism The system by which a country holds lands overseas as possessions. Many colonies were taken from indigenous peoples, held by force, and exploited for their land, mineral wealth, and resources.

constitution A framework of government, laws, and principles. In some countries this is written down in a document and often includes a bill of rights.

emigrants Those who leave their country for another.

ethnic group A group, whether a majority or a minority within a country, whose members share a common and distinct language, religion, culture, and tradition.

fascist A person who holds extreme right-wing political beliefs and is opposed to democracy and liberalism.

genes The elements within the human body that contain instructions for the passing on of certain human characteristics.

geneticist Someone who studies the science of genetics.

genetics The study of the human characteristics that are inborn or passed down as a result of our genes.

guerrilla A member of a rebel army fighting a war against his or her government. Guerrilla soldiers usually fight in small groups, live in hiding, and wear no uniforms.

guest worker A foreign worker who has been invited to work in a country for a fixed period of time and is then expected to leave at the end of his or her contract.

Hispanic Describes people of Spanish or Portuguese descent living in the Americas.

homeland The name given to some rural areas of South Africa where black people were expected to live. These were areas where the land was poor and where there were few jobs.

human rights Rights that include civil (political) rights such as the right to vote. They also include the right to basic human needs such as shelter, food, work, health care, and education.

immigrants Those who enter another country to live.

indigenous people People who have lived in a country from earliest times, for example, the Australian Aborigines and the Native Americans.

migrants People who move from one country to another for economic or political reasons.

Nazi A supporter of Adolf Hitler's National Socialist Party in Germany during the 1930s and 1940s.

neo New, recent, or modern, hence neo-Nazi or neo-Fascist. These people support many of the fascist and racist ideas of Adolf Hitler, especially his hatred of Jews, blacks, and ethnic minority peoples.

prejudice Negative feelings or attitudes toward a group of people that are not based on facts.

race A term used to divide people into groups based on their skin color or other physical or cultural characteristics. "Race" has been shown by many researchers to be a meaningless concept.

racial discrimination The practice of treating people unfairly because of their skin color or ethnic group.

racial harassment Hostile behavior, physical attacks, and intimidation directed at people from ethnic minorities because of their skin color, religion, or culture.

racism Beliefs, actions, and forms of behavior that are based on or motivated by a feeling of racial superiority.

refugee A person who leaves his or her own country because of war, famine, disease, or fear of violence.

segregation The policy of keeping people apart, often on racial grounds.

slavery A system in which one group of people is able to own another group as property and force them to work.

townships Areas on the edge of South African cities where black people were forced to live during the apartheid regime.

United Nations An international organization founded in 1945 after World War II. It is committed to maintaining peace and encouraging cooperation among nations throughout the world.

xenophobia A fear and hatred of foreigners.

BOOKS TO READ

Cozic, Charles P. *Nationalism and Ethnic Conflict* (Current Controversies Series.) San Diego: Greenhaven, 1994.

Dudley, William and Cozic, Charles. *Racism in America* (Opposing Viewpoints.) San Diego: Greenhaven, 1991.

Hays, Scott. *Racism* (Life Issues Series.) Tarrytown, NY: Marshall Cavendish, 1994.

Keene, Anne T. *Racism* (Teen Hot Line Series.) Austin, TX: Raintree Steck-Vaughn, 1995.

Levine, Ellen. *Freedom's Children: Young Civil Rights Activists Tell Their Own Stories.* New York: Putnam's, 1993.

Milos, Ray. *Working Together Against Racism* (Library of Social Activism.) New York: Rosen Group, 1994.

Mizell, Linda. *Racism.* New York: Walker and Co., 1992.

SOURCES

Page 8 The facts in Racism Across the World taken from *New Internationalist* No. 260, October 1994.

Page 11 The quotation from Logan Jack is taken from *Patterns of Racism, Book 2* (Institute of Race Relations, 1982).

Page 14 The quotation from A. Sivanandan is taken from the editorial in *Sivanandan in Europe: Variations on a Theme of Racism, Race and Class* (Institute of Race Relations, 1991).

Page 16 and 21 The figures are compiled from Fekete, Liz and Frances Webber, *Inside Racist Europe* (Institute of Race Relations, 1994).

Page 26 The quotation from Dr. Malan is taken from Birch, Beverly, *A Question of Race* (Macdonald, 1985). The quotation from the Commission of the Dutch Reformed Church is taken from Leach G. *South Africa. No Easy Path to Peace* (Methuen Ltd., 1987).

Page 28 The quotation from Dennis Brutus comes from *The Child is Not Dead—Youth Resistance in South Africa 1976–86.*

Page 29 The quotation from Nelson Mandela is taken from Jean Hayward, *South Africa Since 1948* (Wayland, 1989).

Page 33 The RDP Program is compiled from the ANC's *RDP Reconstruction and Development Programme, A Policy Framework* (Umanyano Publications, 1994).

Page 35 The quotation from Archbishop Tutu is taken from the *Observer*, October 30, 1994.

Page 36 The quotation from Christopher Columbus is taken from *Roots of Racism, Book 1* (Institute of Race Relations, 1982).

Page 39 The quotation from Malcolm X is taken from Small, Steven, *The Black Experience in the United States and England in the 1980s, Racialised Barriers* (Routledge, 1994).

Page 40 The quotation from Maya Angelou is taken from Alibhai, Yasmin and Colin Brown, *Racism* (Wayland, 1991).

Page 46 The facts are compiled from Inglis, Christine, "Race and Ethnic Relations in Australia: Theory, Method and Substance," in Ratcliffe, P. (editor), *Race, Ethnicity and Nation: International Perspectives on Social Conflict* (UCL Press, 1994).

Page 47 and 50 The poems by Bob Randall and Mandjuk Marika are taken from Hicks, D. and M. Steiner, (editors), *Making Global Connections: A World Studies Workbook* (Oliver and Boyd, 1989).

Page 52 The poem by Martin Niemöller is quoted in Supple, Carrie, *From Prejudice to Genocide: Learning About the Holocaust* (Trentham Books, 1993).

INDEX

Numbers in **bold** indicate subjects shown in pictures as well as text.